The Little Book of

TEAM GB

A CIP catalogue record for this book is available from the British Library

Carlton Books Limited
20 Mortimer Street
London W1T 3JW

ISBN: 978-1-84732-852-6

Editor: Martin Corteel
Design: Darren Jordan
Production: Janette Burgin

Printed in China

The Little Book of
TEAM GB

Flying the flag with 170 quick-fire quotes

Edited by Iain Spragg and Adrian Clarke

 Official Product
of Team GB

CARLTON
BOOKS

INTRODUCTION

Ever since the modern Olympic Games were first staged in the city of Athens in 1896, British athletes have lit up the event with some unforgettable performances and dramatic, medal-winning displays.

To commemorate London hosting the Games in 2012 for a historic third time, *The Little Book of Team GB* is a compilation of quotes from British Olympians past and present who have left an indelible mark on the history of the world's greatest sporting stage.

From Eric Liddell being crowned men's 400m champion in 1924 and the two gold medals won by Daley Thompson in the Decathlon, to the legendary Steve Redgrave and his record-breaking five Rowing triumphs, this book of sporting *bons mots* celebrates the very best of Britain at the Games.

'The Olympics have the ability to inspire like no other event on the planet. They inspired me as a young, aspiring athlete and will inspire many, many more when they come to our shores in 2012.'

ROGER BLACK,
silver medallist in the men's 400m at Atlanta 1996,
looks ahead to the London 2012 Games

' Quite simply the Games are the biggest opportunity sport in this country has ever had. It is one that we must not squander. '

LORD COE
urges the country to make the most of London 2012

' The emotion of winning an Olympic gold medal is like getting all your Christmas presents wrapped up in one. You feel every emotion: joy, happiness, relief and pride – pride in being British, pride in winning for the country, pride in winning for yourself and your parents. '

DAVID WILKIE
remembers winning gold in the men's 200m Breaststroke
at Montreal 1976

'A statue of me? With these shoulders?'

REBECCA ADLINGTON,
double gold medallist at Beijing 2008 (in the women's
400m and 800m Freestyle), on the pitfalls of fame

'I've achieved everything I wanted. I have nothing left to prove, including to myself. Looking at what I've achieved, I don't think there's anything that is going to surpass that.'

DAME KELLY HOLMES

reflects on her 800m and 1500m gold medals at Athens 2004 as she announces her retirement in 2005

❛I have plenty of time to be a doctor again, but only limited time to be an athlete and I want gold in London.❜

TIM BRABANTS,
men's Kayak Single (K1) 1000m gold medallist explains why he's putting his medical career on hold to pursue glory in 2012

'I know I can do it. And you know what? When I win gold in London, I'm going to throw that silver I won in Beijing in the bin.'

PHILLIPS IDOWU,
silver medallist in the Triple Jump at Beijing 2008, is
determined to go one better at London 2012

' I live around the corner and see the Stadium every day. That excites me to the limit. Without it, I would have thought twice about going through it all. '

JEANETTE KWAKYE,
sprinter, who has been inspired by the Olympic Stadium
in her recovery from injury

'I have not had the chance to go out there and do myself justice in an Olympic Marathon yet. I have not been able to get to an Olympic Marathon injury-free yet. Hopefully, all this rest will help me have that chance now. I want that chance to stand on the line, having had perfect preparations, to go out there and just do what I enjoy doing best, which is competing when fully fit and in shape.'

PAULA RADCLIFFE
is looking to improve on her 23rd-place finish in the women's Marathon at Beijing 2008

' The feeling of running fast is unforgettable.
The exhilaration you feel running around
a bend, it's like you're in charge,
you're a Ferrari. '

ALLAN WELLS,
men's 100m champion at Moscow 1980, on the
exhilaration of sprinting

16

' You find out a lot about yourself through athletics. If you're cut out to be a winner or a failure or a quitter, athletics will bring it out of you. You're always stripping yourself down to the bones of your personality. And sometimes you just get a glimpse of the kind of talent you've been given. Sometimes I run and I don't even feel the effort of running. I don't even feel the ground. I'm just drifting. '

STEVE OVETT,
men's 800m champion at Moscow 1980,
on the highs and lows of athletics

' Full engagement is what makes the difference between being average and being great in Olympic sport or whatever aspect of life. '

❝ In life you've got a path that if you go down, you'll be successful. A lot of the time in my life I kept coming off that path, whether for my friends, or for football or injury. I just remember watching the athletics in 1995 and thinking I've got unfinished business. I trained and went to the 1996 Olympics and knew that was where I was meant to be. ❞

DARREN CAMPBELL,
a gold medallist in the men's 4 x 100m Relay at Athens
2004, on the challenges he faced in his career

' I never ran to be famous. I only ran to see how fast I could run and to win that gold medal. '

' My most vivid memory of watching sport is going to the 1960 Olympic Games in Rome on a school trip from Malta. My parents told me they couldn't afford it and that we would have to go without a fridge if I went. I did go, we had no fridge and I met Jesse Owens and a young man called Cassius Clay. I got both their autographs. It was a fundamental moment in my life. '

ALAN PASCOE,
silver medallist in the men's 4 x 400m Relay at Munich
1972, reveals how he caught the Olympic Games bug

' If there was a real legacy for 2012, it is to get every young person in the country believing a bit more is possible, not just in sport. '

DUNCAN GOODHEW,
men's 100m Breaststroke gold medallist in 1980, looks beyond London 2012

' The first time I realised the excitement our victory had created at home was when we returned to Heathrow. After landing we were whisked away into a side room for an interview on breakfast television. We were given champagne and didn't even have to get our own luggage. It was just silly. '

SEAN KERLY

remembers Team GB's victory in the men's Hockey
at Seoul 1988

' The gold medals are a great memory. But even the non-medalling games were all very poignant moments in my life. I still close my eyes and put myself there. '

SHIRLEY ROBERTSON,
two-time Sailing gold medallist (in Europe class in 2000 and Yngling class in 2004), reflects on her Olympic career

'It is more than just taking part. I will not simply be turning up for the occasion, but to be chasing a place on the medal winners' podium. Being a part of the London Games is my ambition, winning a medal at my home Olympics is my goal.'

SIMON TERRY,
archer, targets gold in 2012, two decades after he won
two bronze medals at Barcelona 1992

' I honestly think that if the Olympics weren't in London, I wouldn't be sitting here as a badminton player. My will to want to go and play at those Olympics and possibly medal is driving me on. '

NATHAN ROBERTSON,
silver medallist in the Badminton Mixed Doubles at Athens 2004, is inspired by London 2012

'I find Athletics too sexy. I love it – the challenge, the unpredictability. It is like a love affair – exciting, demanding, potentially heart-breaking – but still you do it. If you get it right, it is ecstasy. I can't give up on that, because nothing else gives me that feeling.'

DENISE LEWIS,
the Olympic Heptathlon champion at Sydney 2000,
explains how she fell in love with Athletics

‘ When I lost my world record I took it like a
man. I only cried for ten hours. ’

DALEY THOMPSON,
double Olympic Decathlon champion,
keeps things in perspective

' It's not uncommon that you'll get people embracing, and handshakes and hugs on the medal podium between two people who moments ago were racing for their lives against each other. That's what's wonderful about the Olympics – it's competition without aggression, it is a celebration of sport and I'm so proud it's coming to London. It's going to be wonderful. '

MATTHEW PINSENT,
the four-time Olympic gold medal rower,
sums up the Olympic spirit

' I came away with a certificate for eighth place. I left it in my room in the Olympic Village. I didn't want it. I went there for gold, not a piece of paper for taking part. '

SHANAZE READE,
cyclist, on her disappointment at crashing in the
women's BMX Racing final at Beijing 2008

'Living in the Olympic Village was as special as I thought it would be. Everyone there was at the top of their sport and it was an amazing feeling. It was hot and everyone was in shorts and singlets and we had fun trying to work out what people did depending on their muscles.'

MARY KING,
equestrian legend and silver medallist in the Team event
in 2004, remembers her first Games at Barcelona 1992

' I find other sports a bit boring. In Canoeing the water is always changing, rather than other sports where you are maybe just running in a straight line or Swimming in a straight line. '

LIZZIE NEAVE,
medal hopeful, sings the praises of the
Canoe Slalom

❛If I'm still playing and I'm still considered to make a difference to the team, I'd love to, but if not then I'm definitely going to be there anyway. It's the east end of London, it's on my manor. To be part of getting the Olympics to the east end of London, it's one of the best experiences that I've ever had.❜

DAVID BECKHAM,
football superstar, is still dreaming of playing at
London 2012

' It was very scary. I felt like I had murdered someone and got caught red-handed. I tried not to show those emotions, but that's how I felt on the inside. It was that weird. '

‘ Minority sports in Britain need to be given
a chance to show that they are
just as good as football. Handball is a
fantastic spectator sport and it just needs to
be given a chance. ’

LYNN McCAFFERTY,
British women's Handball captain, champions her sport

' The Olympic gold is the dream. When I watched the Olympics when I was young, I sat there thinking "I want a gold medal". To stand on that podium and hear the national anthem. When you see people in that position you want it to be you and your team. '

KATE WALSH,
British women's Hockey captain, is dreaming of a medal
at London 2012

'I have been on the podium at the Worlds and Europeans but never champion, so they are goals, but I would swap all my other medals for a gold from London.'

EUAN BURTON,
Judo hopeful, is desperate for success on home soil

' Winning a home Olympics would tick all of the boxes and, at 21 years of age, I will then hopefully go on to be one of the greatest of all time. '

AARON COOK,
British Taekwondo star, is aiming high

' The Olympics is, without question, the biggest sporting event in the world. '

ANDY MURRAY,
tennis star, on the importance of London 2012

' It might seem strange when most boys are passionate about football or rugby. But, for some reason, volleyball seemed to light a flame within me. I always wanted to be an Olympian as a child. I just didn't know how. In the end, I found volleyball. '

BEN PIPES,
British men's Volleyball captain, on his personal journey to the Olympic Games

❝ London is the sporting capital of the world. I say to the Chinese and I say to the world, "ping pong is coming home". ❞

BORIS JOHNSON,
Mayor of London, after receiving the Olympic Baton in Beijing in August 2008

' The very moment I crossed the finish line my life changed for ever. Suddenly I was a household name. '

KRIS AKABUSI
reflects on how his life changed after winning silver in the
men's 4 x 400m Relay at Los Angeles 1984

42

‘ When you're in an Olympic final, you're on your own. In other sports you can hide behind a team or be on the winning side but have a rubbish game. Athletics is a fundamentally individual sport and therefore the pressure is greater. ’

ROGER BLACK,
men's 400m silver medallist at Atlanta 1996, on the challenges facing Olympic athletes

' I never thought I would say this but I travel the world and we are now recognised as having the best system in the world which is testimony to, yes, the funding, but also the changes that have been made in British sport. Cycling, rowing, swimming, athletics – it's all a lot more professional than it was in my day. It was run by amateurs and those days have gone. '

STEVE CRAM,
silver medallist in the men's 1500m at Los Angeles 1984,
salutes British sport

' They have bled for this for two years. '

MATT PARKER,
Cycling coach, pays tribute to Bradley Wiggins, Geraint
Thomas, Paul Manning and Ed Clancy after winning
men's Team Pursuit gold at Beijing 2008

'Seeing it for the first time, I was like, "wow!" It looks amazing and usually not that much attention is paid to the outside of the Velodrome – it's usually like a warehouse. This looks totally impressive.'

VICTORIA PENDLETON,
women's Individual Sprint gold medallist in Cycling at Beijing 2008, gives her first impressions of the London 2012 Velodrome

❛I retired once I had got my gold medal. I was at the top of my game. But if I'd had 2012 as my next Games, I wouldn't have had to be asked.❜

DUNCAN GOODHEW,
men's 100m Breaststroke gold medallist at Moscow 1980, on the opportunity to compete in London

' Winning gold was like D-day. I had to face my demons, grit my teeth and ride the best race of my life. And I did it. '

REBECCA ROMERO

reflects on winning Cycling gold in the women's
Individual Pursuit at Beijing 2008

'It was beyond skills almost, it was so primeval. It was just auto-pilot. We were flying blind, rowing blind, we rowed from the heart.'

STEVE WILLIAMS,
rower, on his triumph in the Coxless Four at Beijing 2008

" I was vaguely aware of the history, people tell you about it. But I tried to make it the furthest thought from my mind. And that's why the emotions come out in the end. You bottle it for so long that it just erupts at the end. "

CHRIS HOY
on becoming the first Briton in a century to claim three gold medals at a single Games after winning the Cycling Individual Sprint final at Beijing 2008

'Before Beijing, hardly anyone had heard of us or our sport. Now we're treated like heroes everywhere we go and we're loving it.'

PIPPA WILSON,
gold medal-winning sailor, enjoys the aftermath of her triumph in the Yngling class at Beijing 2008

' This gold medal means the world to us. Like Pippa, I keep mine in my handbag so I can always get it out and touch it, just to make sure it's real. '

SARAH WEBB,
Sailing champion in the Yngling class at Beijing 2008, keeps her gold medal close

' Winning gold was an amazing moment – it's strange. When I've won other events you feel good, but there's still this big urge to be better, to win by more. But when we won gold in Beijing, I knew I was the best and the sense of achievement was great. '

SARAH AYTON,
Sailing gold medallist, on the unique appeal of the
Olympic Games after winning the Yngling class at
Beijing 2008

❛ We just wanted the dream we had as kids to be Olympic champions to come true and there's nothing more powerful than that. It was just emotionally and mentally draining. I dreamt as a kid of standing on the podium and hearing the national anthem. Now that I have experienced it, it is quite a powerful memory to inspire me towards 2012. ❜

MARK HUNTER,
men's Lightweight Double Sculls champion at Beijing 2008, is hungry for more

' God made me fast. And when I run,
I feel His pleasure. '

ERIC LIDDELL,
men's 400m champion at Paris 1924,
reveals his sporting philosophy

' This was the hardest two hours of my life. It's one thing to get to the top of an Olympic sport or to get to the podium. But to stay focused for another four years and try to stay at the top of your sport – especially in the endurance events that I do – it's really tough. I feel more proud and more humble knowing how hard it is to get on the podium and the fact I've done it twice, at two different Olympic Games now, and in two different events. '

DAVID DAVIES

reflects on winning silver in the men's Marathon Swimming 10km at Beijing 2008 – four years after he won bronze in the men's 1500m Freestyle at Athens 2004

' The whole year culminating in the Olympic win is something I treasure as a high point because of the integration of my body and spirit. Everything was in alignment. '

DAVID HEMERY

remembers his victory in the final of the men's
400m Hurdles at Mexico 1968

‘ There is something in the Olympics, indefinable, springing from the soul, that must be preserved. ’

CHRIS BRASHER,
gold medallist in the men's 3000m Steeplechase at
Melbourne 1956, on the spirit of the Games

'Take every superlative there is, roll it into one and you have an idea of the elation I felt when I won the 100m in Moscow. I've never come close to the same emotions since. To achieve something most people can only dream about – the highest accolade in one of the blue riband Olympic events – is a phenomenal thing. Even now I pinch myself sometimes.'

ALLAN WELLS,
sprinter, remembers his famous triumph at Moscow 1980

'If you had told me I'd have won a silver Olympic medal for sprinting six months before I did, I'd never have believed you because until 1947 my sport was the high jump.'

DOROTHY MANLEY
reveals her surprise at coming second in the women's 100m at London 1948

' There's nothing better than running in white shorts, a white shirt, and having a tan to go with my blonde hair. It's a lovely feeling, it really is. You feel as if you're riding in a Rolls-Royce. '

LILLIAN BOARD,
silver medallist in the women's 400m at Mexico 1968, on
the benefits of training hard

' This city provides a wonderful global platform to promote the Olympic Movement, particularly to a young audience. '

LORD COE
hopes London will bring the Games to a new audience

'For all of us it's been a massive inspiration. Now looking forward to 2012, hopefully the success the whole team has had can get the whole nation behind the Games in London.'

BEN AINSLIE,
triple gold medallist sailor (in the Laser class in 2000 and
the Finn class in 2004 and 2008), looks ahead to his fifth
successive Games

' When we stage the Olympics it will inspire kids all over the country. A kid in Scotland or Ireland will be encouraged to take up sport. '

DALEY THOMPSON,
double Olympic Decathlon champion, hopes London
2012 will leave a nationwide legacy

' London has what it takes to host the greatest
sporting show on earth. '

BRADLEY WIGGINS,
three-time Olympic Cycling gold medallist, on the city
hosting the 2012 Games

'There are hurdles to overcome in sport and in life. Sport is a very valuable learning ground for how to live your life in the best possible way.'

LYNN DAVIES,
men's Long Jump champion at Tokyo 1964, on the parallels between athletics and life

' I cannot be frivolous. Winning gold medals at my home Olympics is not only an honour but a duty. '

REBECCA ROMERO,

Cycling gold medallist in the women's Individual Pursuit at Beijing 2008, gears up for London 2012

' Food tastes like cardboard when you're nervous. You have to eat to fuel your body but, as you put the food in your mouth and swallow it, there's no enjoyment from it. In the week before Beijing, I lost about two kilos. '

VICTORIA PENDLETON,
Cycling gold medallist in the women's Individual Sprint at Beijing 2008, on her pre-race nerves

' The public schoolboys tended to stay in their own group so it was up to me as an individual to break that down. The best way to do that was to beat them. It's amazing how, if you beat someone, you are then accepted. '

MARK HUNTER,
rower, on the challenges he had to overcome to win gold
in the men's Lightweight Double Sculls at Beijing 2008

'I want to be the best that I can. If it means doing 120 miles a week or 200 miles a week, I will do everything that it takes.'

MO FARAH,
double European champion, on the sacrifices he'll make
in pursuit of men's 10,000m gold at London 2012

‘ The London Olympics is so inspiring. You've already seen the impact of hosting the Games in my event with the standards getting higher and higher. I'm desperate to be there. ’

LISA DOBRISKEY,
Commonwealth 1500m Athletics champion, on her hopes
for London 2012

'A lot of my greatest performances have been in the UK, so I know it will spur me on to do something special. I'll be needing every person in that crowd to be pushing me through.'

MARLON DEVONISH,
veteran sprinter and men's 4 x 100m Relay gold medallist at Athens 2004, on the benefits of home advantage in 2012

‘ Being a decathlete is like having 10 girlfriends. You have to love them all and you can't afford losing one. ’

DALEY THOMPSON,
double Olympic Decathlon champion, reflects on the demands of his multi-discipline event

' If I see a big fish when I'm swimming, I find it scary. I've always had a fear of them. '

DAVID DAVIES,
men's Marathon Swimming 10km silver medallist at
Beijing 2008, on the pitfalls of competing in lakes

‟ Your stomach feels like the worst stomach ache you've ever had in your life. Your arms are aching and your fingers and your feet are numb. But I like to think my pain threshold is quite high. And you can always see a doctor at the end of the race. ”

KERRI-ANNE PAYNE,
women's Marathon Swimming 10km silver medallist at Beijing 2008, on the agony of the closing stages of a race

' I don't just want to collect medals and say, "Oh, look at me, I'm the Olympic bronze medallist". What does it mean if you can't use it to give back or to inspire somebody else? It's not about medals. It's about how you make a difference to the world. '

TASHA DANVERS
refuses to rest on her laurels after coming third in the women's 400m Hurdles at Beijing 2008

'I don't want to train harder, just smarter. I don't want to lift harder, just cleaner. I don't want to merely run fast, I want to run easy and do it right. I just can't run angry – I've tried. I've never been one to hate my competitors, but that doesn't mean I don't take it seriously.'

MICHAEL BINGHAM,
track star, on his personal philosophy for the men's 400m

‘ I think most pole vaulters are a bit crazy. If you're going to put yourself upside down and over a bar, it's not the most sane of events. But it's definitely one of the most fun. ’

KATE DENNISON,
British record-holder, on the unique challenges of her event

❛ There's a lot of dead time on the start line and an awful lot of noise. Not just the crowd, but the other crews. A lot of other nations go in for this caveman-style grunting. They slap their legs and growl, so there are all these bizarre sounds coming over the water. I don't know whether it's a reflection of our national character, but us Brits don't tend to go in for that. ❜

ACER NETHERCOTT,
cox of the silver medal-winning men's Eight at
Beijing 2008, on a quintessentially British approach to
pre-race preparation in Rowing

'Iain and I were racing against each other aged seven and building Lego when it was too windy to sail, although we were both pretty hopeless.'

ANDREW SIMPSON,
Sailing gold medallist, on his relationship with Star class partner Iain Percy

' I don't believe that I'll realise what I've done until my career is over. I don't think so because we live in such a fast-moving world. You don't have any time for your feet to touch the ground, let alone stop and think about one of the greatest achievements you're probably ever going to have in your life. '

CHRISTINE OHURUOGU
on winning women's 400m gold at Beijing 2008

' Everyone can do the good days. It's the bad days when you step away from your opposition. For me that is sitting in my bed with the alarm going off at 5.30am, continually hitting the snooze button, with the rain and sleet lashing against the window, thinking "I've got to go out in that". But that is the chance to get those eight one-hundredths of a second advantage. They don't come around very often, those opportunities to step ahead. '

STEVE WILLIAMS,
double Olympic Rowing champion in the men's Coxless
Four, on the fine line between success and failure

❝I remember when it was announced we'd got the Games in 2005. It seemed so far away. But now we're talking about it and everyone's excited. Friends ask me if I'm going to be there, but they don't see all the training, the trials, the hard work you have to do to get there.❞

LEON BAPTISTE,
sprinter, refuses to take his place in Team GB for granted

‘ Two different nights, two different events. You can never make up for things, but tonight was special. You have the lows and it puts everything in perspective, but if you win all the time it gets boring. ’

CHRIS HOY
enjoys his Cycling gold medal in the men's 1km Time Trial at Athens 2004, after having had to settle for silver in the Team Sprint at Sydney 2000

' A lot of people have started talking about us getting a podium place in 2012, but us hockey players don't like to blow our own trumpet. '

BARRY MIDDLETON,
Team GB's men's Hockey captain, refuses
to get carried away

' When we are in the Olympic Games, when the gun goes, you are always there to win. You're not going to race for a bronze medal. '

CHARLES VAN COMMENEE,
UK Athletics head coach, won't settle for second-best

'It's like you're living on the edge and you want to scare yourself because that's when you're really living.'

STEVEN LEWIS
on the thrills and spills of the pole vault

' Winning a home Olympics would tick all the boxes, and I will then hopefully go on to be one of the greatest of all time. '

AARON COOK,
Taekwondo medal hopeful, has high hopes for
London 2010

' I know I train much harder than most 400m hurdlers out there. I know there are other people waiting to be number one and that keeps me honest. I ask my coach Malcolm Arnold to bring down fast guys because I don't want to be told I'm the fastest. I want to see it. '

DAI GREENE,
European 400m Hurdles champion, on the hunger required to get to the top

‛I crank up the iPod with Christina Aguilera and the power ballads and crack on. A bit of Tina Turner is always going to get you up for a big race, too. Sometimes it can be a bit hectic trackside before a race, so it's nice to plug yourself in to motivate and concentrate.'

JENNY MEADOWS,
800m star, reveals her pre-race preparations

'I thought it was loud going down the home straight at Crystal Palace, but imagine what that's going to be like in London 2012. It will be incredible. To have a home crowd like that pushing you is a huge incentive. There's no point shying away from it because it's a once-in-a-lifetime opportunity.'

MICHAEL RIMMER,
European 800m silver medallist, is looking forward to home advantage at London 2012

' If we could make a human being capable of curing the world's ills, she would not be a lot unlike Rebecca Adlington. She is honest, hard-working and trusting to a fault. You might even say a bit prim and proper. Just don't get in her way when she's swimming. She gives you nothing. '

BILL FURNISS,
swimming coach, pays tribute to the Beijing 2008
women's 400m and 800m Freestyle gold medallist

' What does it feel like to win an Olympic gold medal? For me it was a shock. It is a relief from the stress, a type of calm. It was two years of work, and in a second it was gone, done. When the medal is put around your neck, it is the realisation of a dream. '

CHRIS BOARDMAN
remembers his emotions after winning men's Individual
Pursuit Cycling gold at Barcelona 1992

❛ We went for a paddle four hours before the race and started hearing our names being chanted at six in the morning. ❜

MATTHEW PINSENT

reflects on the build-up to Britain's Coxless Four victory in the Rowing at Athens 2004

' These days it's not all right to finish anywhere other than first. People see the Olympics in Beijing – it's a high profile event and they just remember that. They think that Team GB wins all the time. '

ED CLANCY,
men's Team Pursuit gold medallist at Beijing 2008, on the increased level of expectation on the British Cycling team

' It was a dream come true for all of us to come together as a team and to take on the Americans and beat them on the greatest sporting stage of all was fantastic. **'**

JASON GARDNER
remembers Team GB's stunning Athletics triumph in the
4 x 100m Relay at Athens 2004

'I don't even know where my medals are. I have no idea. I think one of my nephews had one of them at a school project not long ago. But I've recently moved, so I couldn't begin to tell you where they are.'

LORD COE
has temporarily misplaced his four Olympic medals

❛I couldn't get to sleep until gone 3am.
I was just lying there thinking. I had the
medal next to me. I was so happy. The
first feeling that I had when I woke up was,
"I'm an Olympic champion." It was so
crazy. It was really incredible.❜

NICOLE COOKE,
women's Road Race Cycling gold medallist, remembers
her triumph at Beijing 2008

' I missed my first two Olympics. I didn't get to Barcelona because I broke my shoulder playing rugby. I did get to Atlanta, but the night before the race I developed tonsillitis. It was too late to tell my parents, so they were in the crowd cheering when the boat came out without me. I think it would be fair to say that they panicked. So when it came to Sydney, I felt we had to win. '

JAMES CRACKNELL,
rower, reveals why his Coxless Four gold medal at
Sydney 2000 was so satisfying

'I was always a bit of a show-off and had something where I wanted to express myself. There was something crying out inside me to express myself in sport.'

LYNN DAVIES,
men's Long Jump champion at Tokyo 1964,
explains why he became an athlete

'I tell you the moment that it all really hit home. It wasn't winning the gold, it wasn't when he was standing on the podium, it wasn't the national anthem. Those were all great, but it was later, when he was invited to the Palace to get an MBE and he was allowed to take two guests. He took me and he asked his gran along, my mum, which was a lovely gesture.'

JAMES DeGALE's
father Delroy on the positive impact of his son's Boxing
Middle Weight gold medal at Beijing 2008

' Being an athlete is monastic.
It's like being devoted to God, it's a
single-minded devotion. '

JONATHAN EDWARDS,
men's Triple Jump winner at Sydney 2000, on the
discipline required to become a champion

' The story goes that I am just a normal girl who lived in a council estate who had a passion and a dream and went for it and achieved it in the end. At the end of the day, in anyone's life, people can achieve what they want as long as they are realistic and work hard enough. '

DAME KELLY HOLMES
hopes her women's 800m and 1500m gold medal double
at Athens 2004 will inspire others

‘ To have taken part in one Olympics is an achievement, to have been to five is a phenomenal achievement and there is no reason why she won't be there at the London Games. It really is a tribute to her dedication over two decades and more, and she is a credit to British archery and British sport. ’

JEREMY HUNT MP,
Secretary of State for Culture, Olympics, Media and Sport,
pays tribute to veteran Alison Williamson

'When the first thing anyone asks you is,
"What's it like to play in a bikini?" you
gather what most people think of
this sport over here.'

DENISE JOHNS,
America-based Team GB Beach Volleyball star,
on the preconceptions about her sport

'The fact the girls don't wear much suits the game because that's what you'd wear when you're on the beach. If it attracts a TV audience, that's no bad thing. The more publicity the sport can get the better.'

ZARA DAMPNEY,
Beach Volleyball hopeful, on raising her sport's profile

'There is definitely a role for boxing in our society. It does get kids off the street. I'm happy to be a role model. I never drink, I don't smoke, but I can still go out and have a laugh.'

KHALID YAFAI,
European silver medallist in the Fly Weight division, argues
that boxing can have a positive effect on society

' The 2012 Olympics has been my one and only dream. To represent my country in London is my biggest goal. '

LUKE CAMPBELL,
Bantam Weight Boxing medal hopeful, explains why he has turned down offers to turn professional

' Before the Olympics, I was driving an old Honda Civic and living at home. Now I've got my own apartment and I own a Range Rover Sport and a Jaguar. And celebrity-wise, it's nice to go shopping and be stopped by total strangers asking for a picture or an autograph. '

JAMES DeGALE,
gold medal-winning Middle Weight boxer, reveals the rewards Olympic success can bring

' David Wilkie was somebody who inspired me to become an Olympic champion. In 1976, when I was 12, I saw Wilkie win 200m Breaststroke gold in Montreal. That was critical for me. It was the first time I had connected what I did with something so big. I thought, "I do that, look at that guy. And how brilliant is he? And isn't that exciting? And I do the same stroke as him. Wouldn't it be good to do that?" '

ADRIAN MOORHOUSE,
the men's 100m Breaststroke champion at Seoul 1988, on his sporting inspiration

' I like explaining to people who know nothing about gymnastics that on the bars it also feels like a rollercoaster – except you're in control. If you're on a rollercoaster at Alton Towers, you haven't a clue what's coming next, which is maybe what people think when watching me – is this the routine of her life or is she just going to fall? '

BETH TWEDDLE,
world champion gymnast, on the adrenalin of competing

❛It was a great lifestyle, living by the beach, doing no exercise, having a social life, having fun, being normal. Then I started to think about London 2012. I grew up in the East End and to not be a part of the Olympics would be depressing and criminal, to be watching it on television.❜

MARK HUNTER,
men's Lightweight Double Sculls gold medallist, explains
why he returned to rowing after a year's sabbatical
coaching in America following his triumph at Beijing 2008

‘I was 10 when I started lifting weights in the gym. I liked it straight away and it kept me out of trouble.’

PETER KIRKBRIDE,
Commonwealth Games 94kg Weightlifting silver medallist,
began his career early

'Being a full-time international athlete is a rather peculiar life. I'm abroad a huge amount of time and spend most of my life in a state of extreme fatigue and pressure. Therefore, I can't always be a very good friend. Hopefully, my friends will remember that I'm only an athlete for eight to 10 years. They won't expect more of me than I can give and won't demand anything that compromises my unique lifestyle and strange obsession with moving a boat backwards through the water.'

ANNABEL VERNON,
Rowing silver medallist at Beijing 2008 in the women's
Quadruple Sculls, on her difficult lifestyle choices

' When people talk to me about the Olympics in 2012, I always just have this massive smile on my face. '

JENNA RANDALL,
synchronised swimmer, cannot wait for the
London 2012 Games

' The Olympics inspires so many people, not just us, but junior levels and kids in schools. I think it's really an important time. If the fans are behind us, which I'm sure they will be, great things can happen. '

LIAM TANCOCK,
world champion in the men's 50m Backstroke,
on the impact of the Games

'I still don't think I am any good at what I do and won't until I've won an Olympic gold medal.'

FRAN HALSALL,
Commonwealth Games women's
50m Butterfly champion, wants gold in the
pool at the London 2012 Games

' My grandad got me into it when I was eight to keep me off the streets and to learn how to defend myself. I just fell in love with all the flashy kicks, spins and knockouts. '

JADE JONES,
Taekwondo medal hopeful, was inspired by her family

'When you're a triathlete and you train five hours a day, you eat what you want. Well, that's my rule anyway.'

ALISTAIR BROWNLEE,
Triathlon world champion, eschews a strict dietary regime

'I quite often imagine Hyde Park when I'm running. It's always in my mind if I'm struggling in a session. "Come on, think of Hyde Park. Get through this."'

HELEN JENKINS,
Britain's top female triathlete, can visualise the London 2012 Games

'I'd love it if in 10 years' time, if you said water polo to someone, you wouldn't then have to go and explain what it is. That would be amazing.'

FRAN LEIGHTON
hopes her sport can gain awareness at London 2012

'I just feel proud to come from there,
let alone have something
named after me.'

REBECCA ADLINGTON,
women's 400m and 800m Freestyle gold medallist,
reacts to news a Mansfield pub has been renamed 'The
Adlington Arms' in honour of her exploits in the pool at
Beijing 2008

'It was crazy meeting David Beckham and Jimmy Page from Led Zeppelin. It was just an unbelievable night and it finished off what's been an incredible two weeks for me and for the whole team. It's one night I'll remember for the rest of my life.'

CHRIS HOY
remembers the Closing Ceremony of the
Beijing 2008 Games

' You have to look at the underlying motive for wanting to win. Sometimes it is for the joy of it. Sometimes it's because you want to put other people down. Or sometimes the motive is all down to proving a point. '

STEVE BACKLEY,
double Olympic silver medallist in the men's Javelin
Throw, on the psychology of sport

'When I was 14, Steve Redgrave came to a dinner at Poplar and I got to sit next to him. Seeing his gold medal inspired me.'

MARK HUNTER,
men's Lightweight Double Sculls gold medallist at Beijing 2008, reveals what made him take up rowing

'The night before, I was having dinner with the likes of Seb Coe and Daley Thompson. We all said we'd trade all our sporting achievements for the right result, for International Olympic Committee President Jacques Rogge to say London instead of Paris.'

JONATHAN EDWARDS,
men's Triple Jump champion at Sydney 2004, reflects on
the night before London was awarded the
Olympic Games

'It was the greatest achievement of my professional life.'

SHIRLEY ROBERTSON,
sailor, puts her gold medal in the Yngling class at
Athens 2004 into context

' I think if nothing else, it's shown that belief can enable you to do amazing things and the crazy thing is that we actually did believe going into the final that we could win. '

DARREN CAMPBELL,
sprinter, looks back on Britain's famous victory in the final
of the men's 4 x 100m Relay at Athens 2004

‘ London 2012 is going to be the biggest and best sporting event ever staged in this country, and the anticipation really is growing fast. ’

JONATHAN EDWARDS,
men's Triple Jump gold medallist at Sydney 2000, can feel
the sense of expectation building

129

'I don't think it has sunk in yet. I still feel like the normal Nicole from before the race. But it's just so exciting, a dream come true.'

NICOLE COOKE
struggles to come to terms with her victory in the women's Cycling Road Race at Beijing 2008

'I stood on the podium and heard the national anthem. It was fantastic to have the flag wrapped around me and I was just so proud to be British. It was the happiest day of my life.'

JAMES DeGALE,
boxer, affectionately relives the moment he was presented with his Middle Weight gold medal at Beijing 2008

'It became a head-to-head race. It was no longer the Olympic Games, but me against John Ljunggren. I had to beat him. I'm sure if I'd been thinking all the time that I was on for an Olympic gold medal, I would have lost my focus.'

DON THOMPSON,
the men's 50km Race Walk gold medallist, remembers racing at Rome 1960

' Being selected to compete in any Olympics is the ultimate achievement for an athlete and I have been privileged to enjoy the Olympic experience twice. But to be involved in your own country, supported by home fans, and watched from the stands by family and friends, would be the dream come true. '

SIMON TERRY,
archer, is desperate to compete at London 2012

' It's a relief it's all over. You try to keep your emotions capped through the whole campaign. I've been trying to operate like a robot, but sometimes you're only human. '

CHRIS HOY
lets his emotions get the better of him after winning
Cycling gold in the men's Keirin at Beijing 2008

'It's fantastic news for the sport of weightlifting to be recognised in this way. We're all training hard to make sure we are the athletes chosen to fill those Olympic places.'

PETER KIRKBRIDE,
Commonwealth Games silver medallist, on the
news that up to five British weightlifters will be
in action at London 2012

❛ Looking forward to London 2012, it is important to remember how hard we trained to achieve what we did in Beijing. It's quite easy to look back and think "we won the gold medal, so we can slacken off" and forget how hard it was. ❜

ANDY HODGE,
Rowing gold medal winner in the men's Coxless Four at Beijing 2008, is determined to stay focused

‘I can definitely win a medal at the London Olympics. On my day I know it's possible.’

MO FARAH,
men's European 5000m and 10,000m
champion in 2010, is staying positive

'At one time, I had 50 acupuncture needles in me.'

HARRY AIKINES-ARYEETEY,
sprinter, reveals the lengths he has gone to in order to get fit for London 2012

'I'm sure this makes up for not being an astronaut – on the day, at least.'

DAVID FLORENCE's
father George reveals that his son, a men's Canoe Slalom silver medallist at Beijing 2008, was twice rejected by the European Space Agency

' We all need to grasp the opportunity of the Games being on home soil to inspire our nation to think differently and to include every part of our great nation. '

BARONESS TANNI GREY-THOMPSON
urges the UK to get behind the London 2012 Games

'It's the dream of every athlete to see the Union flag go up at the ceremony and to have a gold medal around your neck. You can't describe the feeling. I finished last in Athens in 2004 and it was the most depressing experience of my life. But it was that, technique, guts and drive that got us across that line.'

MARK HUNTER
reveals how he turned his Athens 2004 despair
into a gold medal in the men's Lightweight Double Sculls
four years later

'I have a picture in my bathroom that helps me keep motivated. It is a picture of a little girl aged about six and she's wearing huge old-fashioned boxing gloves and looking up to a speedball that is way out of her reach above her head.'

GAIL EMMS,
Badminton Mixed Doubles silver medallist at Athens 2004,
reveals her unusual motivational technique

' Swimming is so important to me. I love it and you can't adequately explain to someone else why you love something. To someone else swimming is just swimming, boring, whatever. To me I absolutely love to do what I do and winning gold was a result of training for 365 days a year for 10 years. '

REBECCA ADLINGTON,
double gold medallist at Beijing 2008, outlines
her passion for her sport

' I missed the original MBE slot to get it with the other cyclists so I was surrounded by all these amazing army people and prison officers and I just thought, "What am I doing here? All I've done is ride a bike." Obviously, it's a huge honour for me but I was really nervous when I met the Queen. '

GERAINT THOMAS,
men's Team Pursuit Cycling gold medallist, recalls his visit
to Buckingham Palace after victory at Beijing 2008

'It is important to be nice and solid and my coach puts me through high-pressure training. He has even thrown stones at me, trying to put me off.'

STEVE SCOTT,
Commonwealth Games Double Trap gold medallist, on the unusual training methods employed by the British shooting team

' The statistics say that the most medals are won by people at their second or third Games so hopefully that stat rings true for me. '

EUAN BURTON,
Judo hopeful, is banking that home advantage will pay dividends in London 2012

'My mum played hockey and I said I never wanted to play because standing on the sideline freezing when I watched her was the worst thing ever – but then I tried it and loved it.'

KATE WALSH,
Britain's women's Hockey captain, wasn't an instant
convert to her sport

'For two years, winning at the Olympics propelled my life. Whatever the other girls were doing, I was doing a little bit more. I was an innocent in some ways, but I knew how to get body and mind equipped to win the event.'

ANN PACKER
reveals the extra hours of training required to claim
Athletics gold in the women's 800m at Tokyo 1964

' We had great morale – all the British sailors who raced early on and finished then hung around and cheered the guys still racing. We didn't see that in any of the other teams. '

BEN AINSLIE,
Finn Class Olympic champion at Beijing 2008, thinks team spirit was the key to medal success

' My sport is very much about delivering on the day under a lot of pressure. This means that there is a huge psychological aspect to performing on the day. '

DAVID FLORENCE,
silver medallist in the Canoe Slalom Single (C1) at
Beijing 2008, on the mental demands of elite competition

'When we went to Atlanta in 1996, we were just two years into National Lottery funding and came back with one gold. We started to benefit in Sydney and went on to improve from Athens. What does that tell you? You do not get excellence on the cheap.'

LORD COE
is mindful of the need to invest in sporting excellence

'I came over the line and there was so much. I was just so happy and there were so many emotions coming out all at once. I made so much noise because I guess that's just the person I am.'

NICOLE COOKE

just couldn't contain herself after winning gold in the women's Cycling Road Race at Beijing 2008

‘The last 10 years have come down to six minutes of hell, but it's all worth it.’

ZAC PURCHASE,
rower, reveals it was a long journey to gold in the men's
Lightweight Double Sculls at Beijing 2008

❝Winning that race was a vital part of my education. In part, it formed my character – it made me believe that if I set my mind to something, I could do it. A man's reach should exceed his grasp and mine always did.❞

CHRIS BRASHER

on his landmark victory in the men's 3000m Steeplechase final at the Melbourne 1956 Games

' I've wanted this so badly. I'd beaten everyone in the field so there was a lot of pressure on me to win a medal. I'm "the golden girl of the track". '

' I just concentrated on riding as fast as I could, being absolutely smooth and enjoying myself without anyone to push me off. It helps being positive-nervous, because you've been waiting four years for this. '

EMMA POOLEY,
women's Cycling Individual Time Trial silver medallist at Beijing 2008, on harnessing nervous energy before a race

' School cross-country runs started because the rugby pitches were flooded. There was an alternative – extra studying. This meant there were plenty of runners on sports afternoons. '

GORDON PIRIE,
the men's 5000m silver medallist at Melbourne 1956, on
what 'inspired' him to take up athletics

' You turn up at the Olympics and finish second and you think – you know, I'm really very good. '

JASON KENNY,
Cycling silver medallist, focuses on the positives after
finishing second to Chris Hoy in the men's Individual Sprint
at Beijing 2008

‘ I'm happy I came here and delivered silver for Great Britain. I've been working for this for four years of my life and it feels like heaven. ’

GERMAINE MASON,
Jamaican-born high jumper, revels in his achievement
after finishing second at Beijing 2008

' All top international athletes wake up in the
morning feeling tired and go to bed feeling
very tired. '

BRENDAN FOSTER,
the men's 10,000m bronze medallist at Montreal 1976, on
the trials and tribulations of life as an elite athlete

' I was emotional, scared and nervous. It was absolutely unbelievable. I hope this medal is a stepping stone for British gymnastics. I hope it will inspire youngsters to come into our sport. '

LOUIS SMITH,
Pommel Horse competition bronze medallist at the
Beijing 2008 Games, looks to the future

‘ Every part of your body is hurting. Your stomach is the size of a pea, because all the blood rushes to your arms, your body is saying "Stop", but your head is saying "Come on, keep going". ’

CASSIE PATTEN
went through the pain barrier to claim bronze in the women's Marathon Swimming 10km at Beijing 2008

' Pain is something you expect. You can't win an Olympic final waving at the crowd. '

MATTHEW PINSENT,
four-time Olympic champion rower, sums up his sporting philosophy

❛ It feels like I'm going to wake up in the morning and have to do it all over again. The hardest thing was focusing on the second race and pretending that I hadn't already won one. I have been looking at the gold medal every day and tears have been filling my eyes. I was thinking "Oh my God, I've already got one gold medal and I just want this over and done with". ❜

KELLY HOLMES
on claiming the women's 1500m gold at Athens 2004
– just days after being crowned the women's 800m
Olympic champion

'It has been a busy and confusing time since I got back. You don't know what to expect when you go to the Games, and then you come back and we've had some fantastic opportunities. I went to the GQ awards, which was pretty cool.'

SARAH WEBB,

Sailing Yngling class gold medal winner at Beijing 2008, on the hectic life of an Olympic champion

'This will be a huge opportunity for London to show they can host such an important event. It will be great to have the Games on home ground because my family, friends and all the Olympic fans can enjoy the Games here and it will really add to an already special event.'

BEN AINSLIE,
triple Olympic Sailing gold medallist, on London 2012

'I couldn't believe it. I was optimistic, but it did seem as if we were the underdogs. To come from behind was stunning and Seb Coe's presentation was superb. Completely illogically, I've taken a moment to entertain the possibility of making a comeback. I'll be 43 and will need a new hip and a bionic surgeon.'

STEVE BACKLEY,
two-time men's Javelin silver medallist, was so inspired by London's successful Olympic bid he even considered coming out of retirement

'I'm sure we'll win more medals. Imagine if I'd had that support in Athens, I might have won a gold medal. Hopefully, we'll get more qualifiers and more boxers and finish higher up in the table. I think we'll make one of the best Olympics ever. '

AMIR KHAN,
men's Light Weight silver medallist at Athens 2004, predicts great things for British boxers ahead of London 2012

‘ It's like children – you don't have a favourite. **’**

SIR STEVE REDGRAVE
loves all five of his Olympic gold Rowing medals equally

' Winning this medal was something I didn't even dream about a year ago. The enormity of it all probably won't sink in until the end of the season. '

KELLY SOTHERTON,
heptathlete, comes to terms with her bronze medal at Athens 2004

' It will be an honour to represent my country and get all the kit, stay in the Olympic Village, and, when I'm old enough, get a tattoo with the Olympic Rings. '

TOM DALEY,
diver, already planning his own tribute
to the London 2012 Games

' What I would love to do at the Olympics would be to win with a world record. '

MARY RAND,
long jumper, in the build-up to Tokyo 1964 – an event she
won with a world-record 6.76 metres

'I remember Munich very vividly. It was the most important time of my whole life. I had been competing internationally since 1958, which was when I went to my first Commonwealth Games, and I knew at the age of 33 it was going to be my final competition.'

DAME MARY PETERS

remembers her gold medal performance in the Pentathlon at Munich 1972

'Blink and you miss a sprint. The 10,000m is lap after lap of waiting. Theatrically, the mile is just the right length – beginning, middle, end, a story unfolding.'

LORD COE,
double Olympic men's 1500m champion, extolls the
virtues of middle-distance racing

❛I first thought about competing when I was about 12 and when I was eventually selected it surpassed any of my expectations. There was a special feeling about the Olympics and I still get that buzz today.❜

DAVID OTTLEY,
men's Javelin Throw silver medallist at Los Angeles 1984, on the realisation of a lifelong Olympic dream

' Walking barefoot over wet grass is a most excellent method of hardening and strengthening the feet and it might be as well to mention here that, when circumstances permit, all clothing should be removed for a run round a secluded garden, especially if it be raining at the time. '

GEORGE LARNER
reveals his unusual but hugely successful training regime as the 3500m and 10-mile Race Walk champion at London 1908